The Journey to Self-Love Workbook

An Empowering Self-Esteem Guide For Women To
Build Positive Self-Image, Release Self-Doubt, and
Love Who You Are

By

Cameron J. Clark

This Book Belongs To

_____

_____

Table of Contents

Introduction 1

Prepare To Go On A Journey 2

Exercise 1: How Much Do You Love Yourself? 3

What Do You Want to Achieve? 4

Exercise 2: By The End of This Book, I Want To… 5

Chapter One: Why Do You Feel The Way You Feel? 7

Let's Talk About Social Media & Comparisons 9

Exercise 3: Keep A Journal 11

What About Influencer Culture? 12

Body Confidence Issues 16

Exercise 4: Mirror Check-in 16

Exercise 5: Self Confidence Check In 17

Chapter Two: Even My Insecurities Have Insecurities 19

What Are You Insecure About? 20

Exercise 6: Why Are You Insecure? 21

Overcoming Past Events..22

What Do I Love About Myself?...23

Exercise 7: Accepting Compliments (or Not) 24

Everyone Has Strengths 25

Exercise 8: Your Personal List of Strengths 26

Chapter Three: Talk to Yourself Like Your Own Best Friend........ 29

Why Do You Talk to Yourself This Way?.................................. 30

Exercise 9: Talking To Yourself 30

Consider Your Place in The World 31

Exercise 10: What Should You Say? 37

Chapter Four: Positivity Breeds Positivity 39

The Domino Effect of Positivity.. 40

Exercise 11: Choose the Outcome..41

Get Out Of Your Comfort Zone.. 44

Exercise 12: Creating a Positive Affirmation/Mantra 45

Chapter Five 49

Self-Care Isn't Selfish 49

Self-Care Sunday 50

Exercise 13: Filling Your Self-Care Day..................................50

Exercise 14: Tracking Your 'Me' Time....................................52

It's Time To Be Thankful 53

Exercise 15: Gratitude Journal 54

Mindfulness Meditation & How it Can Help You 54

Exercise 16: Walking Mindfulness Meditation.........................58

Chapter Six: Toxicity is Toxic 59

    You Are Who You Spend Your Time With 60

        Exercise 17: What Are Your Toxic Influences? 61

    Managing The Pain of Toxicity 64

    Three Options: Which Will You Choose? 65

        Exercise 18: Choose Your Route to Free Yourself From Toxicity.............. 66

    The Art of Saying "No"..67

        Exercise 19: The "No" Challenge 67

Chapter Seven: Change Is Scary, But Staying the Same Is Worse.................... 69

    Pushing Back Against Change is Natural 70

    The Story of The Angel & The Devil 70

        Exercise 20: Muting The Devil 71

    Dare To Dream 72

        Exercise 21: A Seat At The Table 74

    Pitfalls On The Way 77

Conclusion 79

4 FREE GIFTS!

Are you ready to embark on a personal transformation journey? As a woman passionate about empowering others, I'm thrilled to offer you 4 free bonus eBooks that will propel your self-development.

By joining my email newsletter, you'll not only receive these valuable eBooks instantly but also gain access to a community dedicated to your growth. Expect personalized weekly tips, heartfelt insights, and empowering resources carefully *curated by me, Cameron J Clark.*

I believe in providing exceptional value to my community, which is why you'll also enjoy exclusive book giveaways, special discounts, and so much more. Best of all, your privacy is of utmost importance to me, and your email address is the only thing I'll ever ask for.

Don't miss out on this opportunity to invest in yourself and join a supportive community of like-minded women. Sign up today, and together, let's uncover the incredible woman within you!

To get your bonus, go to:
https://cameronjclark.com/Free-Gifts
Or scan the QR code below

- Escape the constant barrage of negative messages and take control of your thoughts.
- Transform beliefs into action: Rewire your thinking patterns to overcome self-limiting beliefs and unlock your true potential.
- Counter societal influences: Build self-acceptance, confidence, and resilience in the face of external pressures.
- Tap into ancient wisdom: Discover the timeless practice of affirmations for lasting personal transformation.
- Includes a Free Checklist as a Bonus.

- Cultivate Inner Peace: Discover how acts of kindness can bring inner harmony and serenity, leading to a more fulfilling and joyful life.
- Nurture Authentic Connections: Explore how kindness fosters deeper connections with others, creating a network of support, love, and genuine relationships.
- Boost Your Well-Being: Learn how practicing kindness positively impacts your mental, emotional, and physical well-being, promoting a healthier and happier lifestyle.

- Experience Life-Changing Benefits: Discover how daily gratitude practice can bring happiness, reduce stress, improve relationships, and enhance overall well-being.
- Start a Gratitude Journal: Learn how to begin your gratitude journey by starting a journal to cultivate gratitude, shift your mindset, and invite positivity into your life.
- Deepen with Meditation: Enhance your gratitude practice through meditation, fostering inner peace, appreciation and amplifying the positive effects of gratitude in your daily life.

- Harness the Power of Belief: Discover how cultivating empowering beliefs and positive thought patterns can align your mindset with manifestation, unlocking your true potential for success
- Visualization Techniques: Learn effective visualization techniques to vividly imagine and attract your desired outcomes, amplifying your manifestation abilities and bringing your dreams to life.
- Embrace Abundance Mentality: Shift from a scarcity mindset to an abundance mentality, embracing the belief that there are limitless possibilities available to you, allowing abundance to flow into your life.

Introduction

"One of the greatest regrets in life is being what others would want you to be rather than being yourself." - Shannon L. Alder

How many times have you heard "be kind" lately?

It seems to be a phrase that's doing the rounds, yet the surprising thing is that most of us don't actually extend that kindness to ourselves!

We're all for being kind to those around us, trying to be the best person we can be so everyone else can see how amazing we are, but when it comes to showing yourself a little love and kindness, well, then that concept goes flying out of the window.

Self-love isn't selfish.

I'm going to put that out there now.

It's really not!

When you care for yourself, give yourself the time you need, and show kindness to the most important person in your life (you!), you'll notice your world changes for the better.

After all, how can you look after everyone around you if you don't look after yourself first?

Think about that for a moment!

Prepare To Go On A Journey

"Self-love is an ocean, and your heart is a vessel. Make it full, and any excess will spill over into the lives of the people you hold dear. But you must come first."- Beau Taplin

You've picked up this workbook because you want to revolutionize your life. You want to feel better within yourself and about everything around you.

You've come to the right place!

This workbook is going to help you understand where you're at right now and where you want to be and give you actionable tips to help you get there. We're going to do this together, so don't worry about getting lost along the way.

Self-love is so important for a happy and healthy life. Without it, you'll quickly find yourself slipping into extreme negativity. As such, you won't see opportunities around you, and you'll miss out on everything that life could bring your way.

Confidence helps to open so many doors.

Do you consider yourself confident?

Let's check out just how confident and self-loving you really are.

Exercise 1: How Much Do You Love Yourself?

You can't go on a self-improvement journey unless you know your starting point. Otherwise, how do you know how much work you really need to do?

This quiz will help you work out whether you actually love yourself a lot, a little, or not at all. From there, you know how far you need to go in your journey.

How many of the following statements do you agree with?

1. I am a good person, and I always do my best.
2. I try to see the glass as half full rather than half empty as much as possible.
3. I know I am not perfect, but who is?
4. I have goals I want to achieve in life, and I'm trying to work toward them.
5. When I feel stressed or overwhelmed, I take some time out for myself.
6. I avoid comparing myself to other people because I know no good comes from it.
7. I am good at my job, and it gives me a sense of fulfillment.
8. I try to have a good home and work-life balance.
9. I feel grateful for what I have.
10. I try to eat as well as I can and place priority on sleep.

Results:

If you agree with between 7-10 statements:

You're in a pretty good place already! That doesn't mean you can't benefit from the exercises in this book, but you already have a pretty strong sense of yourself and the importance of self-love. Keep up the good work!

If you agree with between 3-6 statements:

You sit somewhere in the middle. You love yourself to a degree, but there's a lot of room for improvement. The exercises in this book will help you understand why you need to put the focus on yourself a whole lot more to live a healthier and happier life.

If you agree with between 0-3 statements:

You have a lot of work to do, but don't worry! We're about to go on a journey together,

and by the end, you'll have taken several steps on the road to self-love. You've already taken a big step by picking up this workbook, so pat yourself on the back for that!

What Do You Want to Achieve?

Every single person who picks up this workbook will do so for their own individual reasons. There's no one quite like you out there, so it makes sense that you're going to have different goals compared to the next person who picks up this book.

So, before we go any further, what do you want to achieve?

Do you want to become more confident? More positive? Do you want to learn to be more grateful for the things you have? Spend some time thinking about it, and scribble your aims in the section below.

You don't have to write full sentences; nobody else is going to read this but you—unless you want someone to!

Exercise 2: By The End of This Book, I Want To…

_____

_____

_____

_____

_____

_____

_____

_____

_____

_____

_____

_____

_____

_____

_____

_____

_____

_____

_____

_____

Check back on your goals as you move through the chapters and see how close you are to achieving your aims listed above. Whenever you see that you're on your way toward reaching them, celebrate a little! It's important to celebrate every small win because, let's face it, this isn't an easy journey to go on.

But don't worry; I'm here to help you every step of the way.

Chapter One

Why Do You Feel The Way You Feel?

"Your self-worth is determined by you. You don't have to depend on someone telling you who you are." - Beyonce

From time to time, everyone struggles with self-confidence. For some, it's just a temporary thing, usually as a response to a negative event in their lives.

Maybe they lost their job, broke up with a long-term partner, or simply found themselves struggling for another reason. However, once a period of time has passed, that negative feeling slowly ebbs away, and the person starts to feel much more like their old self again.

But what if it continues and that new feeling becomes their new self instead?

It's time for an intervention, that's what!

In this chapter, I want to explore why you feel the way you do. You already know your starting point, and you might have a few ideas about what has led you to this point already. If you don't have a clue, spend some time brainstorming.

Can you think of anything?

If you can, scribble it down here:

_____

_____

_____

_____

_____

_____

_____

_____

_____

_____

_____

_____

_____

_____

_____

_____

_____

_____

_____

_____

_____

_____

_____

_____

_____

_____

_____

_____

_____

There are so many things in life which affect the way we see ourselves. Some come from within, and some are more external, but do you know what? You have more say over them than you think.

Let's take a look at a few different potential causes, one by one. As we move through them, consider whether that particular cause might be a reason for you feeling so negative about yourself.

Remember, self-image and self-worth are so closely linked that it's impossible to raise one without the other. When you think about yourself positively, you feel like you're worth more. When you feel negative about yourself, you don't feel like you're worth very much at all—but remember, you're worth the world!

"Rock bottom became the foundation on which I rebuilt my life." –
J.K.Rowling

Let's Talk About Social Media & Comparisons

Most people use social media these days, and it's great for so many things. We can keep in touch with people far away, share inspiring things, and keep up-to-date with everything that's happening in the world. But what about the downsides?

It's true that social media has changed our lives in many positive ways, but it has also brought a very toxic element our way, too.

Ask yourself these questions and answer them honestly:

- Do you always post the truth on social media?

- Do you think other people always post the truth on social media?
- Have you ever been bullied or received negative comments via social media?
- Do you use social media to follow old friends or exes?
- Does social media ever make you feel negative about your own life, perhaps as if you're lacking in some way?

Few people post the truth on their social media pages, and I'll tell you why. We all want approval. There is a huge part of society that simply seeks validation, and it's just not healthy. The only person you should seek validation from is yourself; if you're always looking for other people to like your pictures or tell you how amazing you are, well, you have more work to do than you realized!

When you see posts on social media that stretch the truth, you start to compare your own life to theirs. Perhaps you see your friend posting about an amazing vacation with their partner. They're both smiling, laughing, and looking amazing, with a stunning sunset behind them.

On the surface, it looks great, right?

Well, perhaps not.

You see, prior to that photograph being taken, it's possible that they had an argument, they weren't really speaking to one another, but they wanted to post a great picture, so they pasted on smiles and looked adoringly at the camera. The sunset? Well, that just happened to be there. Once the picture was posted, they probably didn't speak for the rest of the evening because they were still seething from the argument they had.

Oh, and as for looking amazing, they filtered the life out of the photo before posting it.

And you're comparing yourself to this fakery!

"Comparison is the thief of joy." – Theodore Roosevelt

The other issue: following people who we simply shouldn't follow. Are you still friends with an ex-lover or ex-friend, and do you use social media to keep an eye on them? That right there is pretty negative behavior, and it will cause you to compare your life to theirs or compare how they portray their current lives to how their lives used to be with you in them, leading to all sorts of potentially negative feelings. And again, how do you know they're posting the truth?

Exercise 3: Keep A Journal

For two weeks, keep a diary/journal and note down how many times you feel negative when you use social media of any kind.

Particularly keep an eye out for:

- **Patterns** – Is there a particular person or subject that makes you feel more negative than others?
- **Triggers** – Or is there a person or subject that triggers you into feeling a specific emotion? Write it down and try to go into as much detail as possible on what you're feeling.

After two weeks, sit down with a coffee and look through your diary/journal. Can you see any patterns emerging or clear triggers?

These are things you need to try to handle in one of the following ways:

- **Avoid** – Avoiding a subject can often be difficult, but in some cases, it might be necessary. If it's a particular person, you can block them on your social media accounts.
- **Minimize** – This means you try to see less of this person or subject. You can often set filters on social media, which will help you see less of what bothers you.

- **Face** – This is the best option, although the hardest. Face whatever bothers you and work out why. What can you do to overcome this issue?

Carry on with your diary/journal for another two weeks and repeat the process. Have you made any progress?

What About Influencer Culture?

Alongside social media, we have influencer culture, and this is even worse for causing comparisons.

What does an influencer do? What is their job description?

An influencer's job is to influence a person into doing a certain thing or buying certain products.

So, comparisons are part of the deal, right?

Do you have influencers you always watch on Instagram, TikTok, or YouTube? If so, scribble them down below.

_____

_____

_____

_____

_____

_____

_____

_____

_____

_____

_____

_____

_____

_____

_____

_____

_____

_____

_____

_____

_____

_____

_____

_____

_____

_____

_____

_____

_____

_____

_____

_____

Now, what are the good things about watching these people, and what are the bad?

For instance, if you watch a beauty influencer, do they make you feel good about yourself? Or do they make you feel guilty, so you follow their advice in the hopes of looking like them?

In the space below, write the pros and cons of watching each of the creators listed above. If you have more than one, repeat the exercise for each.

Pros:

_____

_____

_____

_____

_____

_____

_____

_____

_____

_____

_____

_____

_____

_____

_____

_____

_____

_____

_____

_____

_____

_____

_____

_____

_____

_____

_____

Cons:

_____

_____

_____

_____

_____

_____

_____

_____

_____

_____

_____

_____

_____

_____

_____

_____

_____

_____

_____

_____

_____

_____

_____

_____

_____

Is this person a good influence on you? If you're seeing more cons than pros, perhaps you should switch channels and find an influencer who makes you feel positive about yourself.

Body Confidence Issues

"Feeling confident, being comfortable in your skin – that's what really makes you beautiful." – Bobbi Brown

It doesn't matter who you are—you probably have certain parts of your body you really don't like. When you look in the mirror, you probably pick at the things you don't like and totally overlook the good parts.

Isn't it time we started to be a little more positive about the bodies we have? After all, you'll only get one, so you might as well appreciate it!

Society has somehow conditioned us to believe that there is only one type of acceptable body and that everyone else needs to change themselves to fit in. That's absolute trash. There are a million and one different body types, and every single one of them is more than acceptable.

Exercise 4: Mirror Check-in

This exercise might make you feel a little uncomfortable at first, but stick with it. Learning to love your body is a journey that takes time, but the longer you stick with it, the easier it will become.

I want you to stand in front of the mirror, either naked or in your underwear. Close your eyes for a few seconds, take a few deep breaths, and when you're ready, open your eyes.

Force yourself to look at your body. Start at your toes and work your way up to the top of your head. Make sure you don't rush or skip over any body part. You need to look at every single thing.

Now, you're sure to come up with some negative ideas as you do this. So, instead, you're going to reframe them.

For every single part of your body that you notice a negative comment springing up in your mind, do this:

- Tell yourself "NO!" and mentally visualize your hand pushing the negative comment away. It might be useful to visualize the comment as a black ball or something else that connects with you. You can say the word aloud if it helps, but be very forceful as you mentally push it away.
- Now, take a deep breath again and replace that negative comment with a positive one. For instance, if you think, "I have big feet," replace that with, "My feet help me get around all day long."
- Repeat the process for every part of your body that concerns you.

It's a good idea to repeat this exercise once per week to really solidify the reframed thoughts in your mind. Over time, you'll slowly notice your body confidence grow.

Exercise 5: Self Confidence Check In

Low self-confidence has the power to ruin your life. Being confident doesn't mean being arrogant; it just means being grateful for what you have in your life and believing in yourself.

To prove just how powerful self-confidence can be, I want you to think of three instances when low self-confidence affected your life in a negative way. Perhaps you felt too shy to ask out someone you really liked, or you didn't believe in your ability to get a job, so you never went for it.

Write down three examples below.

1.

2.

3.

For each experience, think about the negative connotations that issue brought to you. If you didn't ask someone out because you were too shy, what happened? Are they now with someone you know, and you have to watch them every day?

Now try and think of what would have happened if you hadn't allowed your lack of self-belief get to you and you would have just gone for it.

Can you see the difference and how low self-confidence holds you back?

Now, make a vow to change all that for the better.

Chapter Two

Even My Insecurities Have Insecurities

"There is no such thing as perfect security, only varying levels of insecurity." – *Salman Rushdie*

Every single person on this planet has insecurities. Even Beyonce has insecurities—yes, it's true! The fact of the matter is that some people simply hide them better than others, and some people simply don't allow them to stop them from living their best lives.

You'll never get to the point in your life where you have no insecurities or hang-ups whatsoever. It's just not possible. Don't try and aim for that type of perfectionism because you'll only end up setting yourself up to fail. Instead, aim to make peace with your insecurities and stop them from letting you go for what you want.

You design the life you want, not your insecurities.

The secret is not to focus on the things you don't like about yourself that much or the things that make you feel scared or down. It's about instead focusing on the positives and the things that bring you joy. It's an extension of the exercise you did in the last chapter when you stood in the mirror and changed your negative thoughts into positive ones.

It's very easy to feel alone when you're drowning in insecurities, but it's important to remember that everyone around you feels the same to some degree.

What Are You Insecure About?

It's brainstorming time!

What are you insecure about? When you're coming up with this list, don't just focus on your body or appearance; think about your life as a whole. Write down everything you can think of below.

_____

_____

_____

_____

_____

_____

_____

_____

_____

_____

_____

_____

_____

_____

_____

_____

Exercise 6: Why Are You Insecure?

From the list of insecurities you've written above, take each one in turn and think about why you're insecure about that thing. What led you to that point in your life?

Are you insecure about it for a good reason, or are you insecure about it because you think you should be?

Answer the following questions for each insecurity you have:

- Why am I insecure about this?
- What happened in the past to lead me to feel this way?
- What concrete evidence do I have that proves I need to feel negative about this thing?
- How can I face this insecurity and reduce its control over me?

Most insecurities are rooted in fear. We worry about what 'might' happen without really focusing on the fact that it's very unlikely to come to fruition. As a result, we start to avoid a situation completely because we're terrified of coming face to face with that particular event or thing and failing.

But what if you didn't fail? What if nothing happened at all?

You see, insecurities are nothing but an illusion. If you're insecure about your ability to do your job, do you have proof that you're actually terrible at what you do? If you're that bad, why are you still employed? Instead, you're likely just scared of what might happen if you one day find yourself without work, and you're worried about how you would cope.

It's just a fear that's developed into an insecurity.

If you're insecure about your body, ask yourself if it really matters. Why do you think that other people don't find you attractive? Do you have actual concrete proof that every single person walking on the planet doesn't like you because of how you look?

Of course, you don't!

It's a fear of being found unattractive that is fueling your insecurity.

Overcoming Past Events

"Fear is the path to the Dark Side. Fear leads to anger; anger leads to hate; hate leads to suffering." – Yoda

It's possible that something happened in the past that has caused you to develop an insecurity in the here and now.

Look, bad stuff happens; it's part of life. You can either live your life focused on the past or learn from it and move on. You can improve and do better in the future.

For instance, if you previously made a mistake at work and it put you into a bad situation in your job, you might be terrified of making the same mistake again. As a result, you're really insecure about your work-related abilities, and you're always on edge.

It's understandable, but what can you do to fix it?

You can analyze that mistake and learn what you did wrong so you can make sure you don't make the same mistake again.

Life is a constant learning curve, and the more we learn, the more we avoid repeating old patterns and mistakes.

Of course, it could be that you're insecure about something that someone said to you in the past. Now, remember that people can be horrible sometimes. Really horrible.

If someone told you that you were overweight or unattractive, ask yourself why they did that. You might think that they said it because it's the truth. No! It's more likely that they were feeling bad about themselves, and they were deflecting their insecurities onto you. People like to drag others down because, somehow, it makes them feel better about themselves.

Twisted, right?

You could be beating yourself up in the present because of something a person said to you in the past, someone who was beating their own self up in the first place.

Using the list of insecurities you wrote down earlier in this chapter, identify whether any of them were due to an offhand comment from another person. If you find one that was, push that aside. Unless this person is a high authority on the subject (very unlikely), then what they say in the heat of a moment is worth nothing at all.

What Do I Love About Myself?

We always find it very easy to pick holes in ourselves and talk about the things that we don't like, but if someone asks you to name a few things you like about yourself, you might find that you need to think about it for a second.

Ask yourself this: do you find it hard to list your best friend's good points? Probably not. You're probably all too keen to let them know how they always have shiny hair, they're intelligent, and they have a great sense of humor. But when it comes to listing your own plus points, you're left with a blank page.

Exercise 7: Accepting Compliments (or Not)

One very common issue in people with low self-esteem and a million and one insecurities is the inability to accept a compliment.

Which of these is true for you?

a) If someone gives me a compliment, I smile and say thank you.
b) If someone gives me a compliment, I mutter a thank you and think that they're just being nice; they don't really mean it.
c) If someone gives me a compliment, it makes me really uncomfortable, and I retort back with a self-deprecating comment.

Let's pick each of those responses apart.

If you chose A:

If—hand on your heart—you can say that you do this regularly, you're in good shape. People give us compliments because they mean it. Nobody is going to go out of their way to compliment you if they don't mean it; they're far more likely to use a sarcastic tone, which you'll be able to spot immediately.

So, if you can smile and thank them, make sure you keep on doing it. And, while you're in the process of doing so, be sure to pay forward the good deed by complimenting them and making their day in return.

If you chose B:

The fact you thanked them is good, but the fact that you think they don't mean it is pretty negative. As I've just mentioned, the overwhelming majority of people give compliments because they mean them. Why do you think this person wants to be deliberately mean?

The next time someone gives you a compliment, carry on with the "thank you," but stop yourself there. Don't allow yourself to think anything else. If that 'they don't mean it' thought tries to peek through, push it away, and think of something else quickly. The more you do this, the less that thought will occur and bother you.

If you chose C:

You might think that self-deprecation is a form of humor, but it's actually really damaging. You're putting yourself down for someone else's comedic benefit. Why do you feel you need to do that?

If a person has given you a compliment, you don't need to try and prove them wrong. By doing so, you're basically throwing their compliment back in their face.

The next time someone gives you a compliment, smile, say "thank you," and don't go any further. Bite your tongue if you need to—just not too hard. If there is an awkward silence afterward, don't feel the need to fill it; just change the subject if necessary. Avoid reframing their positive compliment back to a negative.

Everyone Has Strengths

"How you love yourself is how you teach others to love you." – Rupi Kaur

Believe it or not, you have a large number of positive points about yourself and

strengths that make you who you are. Yes, you have weaknesses, but so does everyone. Even the most famous and successful people on the planet have weaknesses.

There is literally not one single person on this planet of ours that can honestly say they don't have one weakness at all.

If they do, they're lying in a big way.

You might think that you should focus on improving your weaknesses because that would allow you to cut down on your insecurities, but it's actually better to focus on your strengths instead. That way, you'll be unstoppable.

So, what are your strengths?

You've got a blank canvas in your mind, haven't you?

It's the same as when you try to think of something good about your appearance—you can't think of anything. But negative? Oh, there's a whole list!

Exercise 8: Your Personal List of Strengths

When you focus on your strengths, it doesn't mean that you're ignoring your weaknesses; you're well aware that they exist; you're just choosing not to dwell on them too much.

For instance, if you know that you're not the best dancer in the world, but you're great at singing, you'll just choose to sing more than you dance, right? That's basically what this is about. Doing more of the good stuff and keeping the other things to a minimum.

But first, you need to know what you're good at. Although you might be able to come up with one or two things, this is going to take some deep thinking. So, let's move onto our next exercise.

- **Step 1** – Every single day, write down three things you're good at or things you like about yourself. You must choose three. If you can think of more, write them down, but it shouldn't be any less than three.
- **Step 2** – Repeat the process for one full week.
- **Step 3** – After seven full days, sit down with the list and really pay attention to

what you've written. You'll probably be feeling a little more confident by this point, so is there anything else you can add?

- **Step 4** – Look at how you can do more of the things you are good at. For instance, if you're good at photography, are there opportunities in your life to do more of it? Could you extend your hobby or even make a living from it? Or, if you're good at making people laugh, can you get together with your friends more often and spend more time being sociable and fun?

The more you focus on your strengths and the things you like about yourself, the less your insecurities matter. In a short amount of time, you might notice that those things that bothered you so much before don't bother you at all now.

Chapter Three

Talk to Yourself Like Your Own Best Friend

"I may be alone, but I am never lonely. I am always with my best friend, and that is me." – Debasish Mridha

Every single day, there is a constant stream of chatter going through your brain. No, it's not from the radio, TV, or people outside; it's you talking to yourself.

Don't worry; you're not going mad—everyone does it!

There's no issue if the musings going through your mind are positive and fun. However, it's a huge problem when they're negative.

In the end, you become what you tell yourself.

If you constantly tell yourself that you're useless, even if you have absolutely no proof to back up that claim, you'll feel that you're useless. If you always tell yourself that you're ugly, even if you're clearly not ugly, you'll convince yourself that you are.

The power of the mind is extreme, and it's important to harness it in the right way to avoid going down a very dark road indeed.

Why Do You Talk to Yourself This Way?

Would you ever dream of telling your best friend that they're useless and ugly? No! You wouldn't tell them that even if you secretly believed it to be true!

So, why do you think it's okay to talk to yourself in this way?

At the end of the day, the only person who will always be with you through thick and thin, rain or shine, is you. You have to be your own best friend because you're with yourself 100% of the time. Would you consider spending 100% of your time with another person that you really didn't like that much? Of course, you wouldn't!

You have a choice here: you can choose to love yourself, or you can carry on living in misery. Because being someone you don't like is miserable.

The bottom line is that negative self-talk is extremely damaging, and it's time we all became more aware of the constant stream of chatter that goes through our brains every single day.

Exercise 9: Talking To Yourself

This exercise is going to take a lot of self-awareness, and you might find that at the end of just one day following it, you're pretty tired. For sure, it's exhausting trying to be aware of as many of your own thoughts as possible. But by doing that, you can work out just how much of a negative self-talk problem you truly have.

You won't catch every single thought, but try and catch as many as you can. When you notice that you're telling yourself something negative, label it as such and ask yourself why you're doing it. What proof do you have of what you're telling yourself?

You'll find pretty quickly that you have no proof whatsoever, and you're just feeling full of negativity for no good reason at all.

Consider Your Place in The World

"It's your place in the world: it's your life. Go on and do all you can with it, and make it the life you want to live." – Mae Demison

We all have a place in the world. When you're lacking in self-confidence, it's easy to feel like you're just existing that you're not really contributing anything of note. But the truth is that you are—you just can't see it.

There are people who love you, tasks you complete every day that make someone else's life easier and contribute to the smooth running of a process, and you have a role to play in the world at large.

Being proud of what you do and what you contribute is important, but we often tell ourselves that what we do is no big deal. It *is* a big deal! Everything you do with your time is done voluntarily and requires effort; how can it not be a big deal?

What is your role in life? I'm not talking about your job title but the roles you play in general. Are you a spouse? Parent? Partner? Friend? Colleague? Volunteer? Guardian? Animal lover? What are you? There are bound to be several things you come up with; write them down here:

Whenever you find yourself feeling low or simply having a bad day, look back over that list, and you'll see just how important you are to the world and just how many roles you play every single day.

But of course, you might find that there are other roles you want to play that aren't in your life right now. If that's the case, it's your life to design! Make those roles a part of your life and find opportunities to keep going further.

If you want to volunteer and make a difference in a particular cause, find out how you can do that and go for it. If you want to spend more time with your friends, set aside some time in your schedule and coordinate when they are free.

Inactivity simply makes you wish you could do more, and then you start to feel bad about the fact that you're not doing what you want. I'm sure you can imagine that this is fertile ground for regret.

And that leads to "what if."

Nothing good ever comes from "what if."

All you end up doing is feeling bad about the fact you didn't do something or that you did something you wish you didn't. But can you go back and change it? No! You cannot turn back the clock; all you can do is learn from the experience and do better next time.

Is there any event or non-event in your life that you often sit and think 'what if' about? Write it down here:

_____

_____

_____

_____

_____

_____

_____

_____

_____

_____

_____

_____

_____

_____

_____

_____

_____

_____

_____

_____

_____

_____

_____

_____

_____

_____

_____

_____

_____

_____

_____

_____

_____

_____

_____

_____

_____

_____

Now, what can you do to learn from that issue to prevent the same regret in the future?

_____
_____
_____
_____
_____
_____
_____
_____
_____
_____
_____
_____
_____
_____
_____
_____
_____
_____
_____
_____
_____
_____
_____
_____
_____
_____
_____
_____
_____
_____

"Your life is a book; make it a bestseller." – Shanon Grey

If there is something you want to do, but you can't do it right now, make a plan. For instance, maybe you want to change your career, but you don't have the training. In that case, what can you do to get that training? Do you need to go back to school? Can you take a night class? How about reaching out to someone prominent in that area and asking them to be your mentor?

Negative self-talk often comes from inactivity. If you want something, the only person who can get it is you.

So, let's do some more writing. What do you want in life? Scribble a few ideas down and decide how you can start the wheels in motion.

_____

_____

_____

_____

_____

_____

_____

_____

_____

_____

_____

_____

_____

_____

_____

_____

_____

_____

Exercise 10: What Should You Say?

We know that we often speak more kindly to other people than we speak to ourselves, but do you understand just how big of a problem this is?

Let's look at some examples so you can see how negative self-talk is never the right answer.

Scenario 1: You're having a bad hair day.

What should you do?

a) Wash it immediately; you can't go out with bad hair, people will make comments.

b) Style it as best you can and decide you'll wash it later on when you get home.

c) Feel about your hair all day and tell several people about how bad your hair is.

The answer: B. Okay, so your hair matters, but you can style it out for a day, right?

Why the others are wrong: If you care so much about people commenting on your hair, that's quite a negative outlook. And if you constantly tell people that your hair is bad, you're being self-deprecating, and that's equally as negative.

Scenario 2: You make a mistake at work. Although it's not a huge mistake, you feel terrible about it.

What should you do?

a) Look at what you did wrong and learn how you can avoid doing it again.

b) Apologize profusely to your colleagues and explain that you're having a bad day.

c) Allow the stress of the situation to stop your productivity for the day as you constantly tell yourself how stupid you are.

The answer: A. Okay, so it's not ideal, but everyone makes mistakes. That's how we learn. Just figure out what you did wrong, and don't make the same mistake twice.

Why the others are wrong: Telling your colleagues that you're sorry for the mistake isn't bad, but trying to explain it away with a 'bad day' excuse means you're not taking ownership of the mistake. Constantly telling yourself that you're stupid and allowing yourself to become stressed will only make the day worse and make it even more likely that you'll make more mistakes.

Scenario 3: You accidentally forget your friend's birthday.

What should you do?

a) Call your friend immediately and admit that you forgot. Apologize for being a terrible friend and beg for forgiveness.
b) Panic and then make a joke on social media about forgetting their birthday, hoping that they see the funny side.
c) Send your friend a belated birthday gift with an apology and arrange to take them out later that week.

The answer: C. It might seem obvious, but you'd be surprised how many people try to deflect the blame with humor. Own up to your mistake and show that you're truly sorry with a gift and an offer to make it up to them. You don't need to grovel.

Why the others are wrong: Admitting that you forgot isn't a bad thing, but you're not a terrible friend for forgetting. You really don't need to beg. And joking about it won't put you in your friend's good books because it looks like you're not taking it seriously.

In all of these examples, you can see that the negative self-talk or self-deprecation route is never the right choice. Instead, admit your mistakes or shortcomings, be proactive, and look to the future. It's the single best way, every time.

Chapter Four

Positivity Breeds Positivity

"There is always light, if only we're brave enough to see it. If only we're brave enough to be it." – Amanda Gorman

Do you see the glass as half full or half empty?

You might think that how you see the world is a default setting, but you can choose how you see that glass. It's all up to you.

If you see it as half full, you're grateful for what's left. If you see it as half empty, you're lamenting what's been lost and what you don't have.

Can you see how one is positive and one is negative?

For sure, the human brain is actually designed to be negative, but it's not a switch that can't be moved to the other direction. The brain does this because it's trying to keep you safe. Back in the days when huge predators were roaming the planet and cave people were trying to survive, everything was a threat. They needed to always be on high alert to make sure they didn't end up as a wild animal's lunch.

So, the brain developed the "fight or flight" response. This means whenever it sees something that it deems to be a threat, it kicks into action and gives you what you need to fight it or run away very fast. The best way for it to do that was to see everything as a threat, to be constantly negative.

The good news is that we no longer need to run away from mammoths and saber-toothed tigers, and we no longer need to be constantly negative just to survive. So, it's time to go against years of conditioning and turn that switch off.

The Domino Effect of Positivity

"A positive mindset brings positive things." – Philipp Reiter

The ironic thing about positivity is that once you start on that path, it brings other positive events into your life. No, it's not magic, but it might feel a little like that.

When you start to see the world as a brighter and more positive place, you see opportunities everywhere. If your mind is stuck in the doldrums and you're negative all the time, you won't see these chances because you're so focused on how terrible your life is. The opportunities are still there in front of you, but you're blind to them.

However, once you start to open your eyes to the wonders of the world, they'll suddenly materialize before you. Of course, it's still up to you to take those chances and work toward achieving them, but the fact you can see the potential around you is a major plus point!

When was the last time you took a small risk?

I'm not talking about big or reckless risks; I'm talking about small risks that could change the course of something in your life. Can you remember the last time?

Let's explore this a little.

Exercise 11: Choose the Outcome

Often, when you take a chance in life, it breeds other chances. Your confidence grows, and more opportunities come your way. It's a domino effect.

But it all comes down to you taking the chance.

Scenario 1: You're feeling stuck and a little bored in your current job, and you'd like to feel energized and excited about your work. What do you do?

a) Feel grateful for the fact you have a job and simply carry on as normal.

b) Check job advertisement boards online but decide that you lack skills and experience and are better off staying where you are.

c) Speak to your manager about the possibility of extra responsibilities and voice your desire to work toward a promotion.

Why is A incorrect? It's good that you have a job, but unless you do something to change your situation, you'll always be dissatisfied. Work isn't only about money!

Why is B incorrect? It's good that you showed initiative by looking at job adverts, but you allowed your lack of self-confidence to stop you from moving forward. Take the next step!

Why is C correct? You're taking the initiative and a chance! Your manager may not know that you're feeling this way, but by talking to them, you're opening up a world of potential opportunities.

What might come from taking the correct action? Your manager may give you extra responsibilities that will help you learn new skills. When a promotion opportunity arises, you'll be best placed to go for it, and your confidence will rise in the process.

Scenario 2: You've admired the barista in your local coffee shop from afar for a while now. You have polite conversations, and you feel like they always pay more

attention to you than anyone else. You want to see if they like you back, but you're scared of rejection. What do you do?

a) The next time you have a conversation, steer the chat toward their personal life and try to inquire whether they have a partner.

b) It would be too awkward to ask out the barista in case they say "no." You like that coffee shop and don't want to have to find another.

c) Be bold and ask them out for a meal.

Why is B incorrect? If they say "no," so what? You're both adults; you can use it as a platform to build a platonic friendship instead! And if not, there are many other coffee shops you can try.

Why is C incorrect? Taking bold action isn't always wrong, but if you don't know whether this person is already in a relationship or not, you're risking a little too much. But well done for showing confidence!

Why is A correct? This is a subtle yet successful approach! You'll get to find out whether they're attached or not, which allows you to decide whether to then ask them out or not. Plus, inquiring about this will show the barista that you're interested.

What might come from taking the correct action? If you find out that they're single, you can then suggest going out for a drink or a meal sometime. If you find out they're not single, you can still be friends with this person.

Scenario 3: You want to change direction in your career to something totally different, but people around you tell you that you're crazy to try. What do you do?

a) Decide that they're probably right; it would be too time-consuming anyway.

b) Do some online research about training you can do in your own time.

c) Quit your job and go for it. Life is too short.

Why is A incorrect? It may be time-consuming, but you might end up with a career that you take great pride and satisfaction from. Isn't it worth trying?

Why is C incorrect? Changing career direction often requires re-training and mentorship. Quitting your job and expecting to simply walk into your new career is a bit arrogant.

Why is B correct? You can train for your new career while still earning money in your current job. That way, you're taking small steps toward the change you want to make, and you'll be better placed to apply for jobs once you have the necessary skills and qualifications.

What might come from taking the correct action? If you take an evening class or even an online class, you'll be able to meet people who are in the same potential career area as you. You can pick their brains and learn more, plus you might meet new friends and have more networking opportunities. While doing this, you're still earning money, which will help to fund your career move.

Scenario 4: You're tired of renting your small house and would love to move into your own larger spot, but it's very expensive, and you've never been a very good saver. What do you do?

a) Be grateful you have a roof over your head, and remember all the times you tried to save up money in the past and failed. Due to that, you stay where you are.

b) Look into homeowner loans and other options that may allow you to access a deposit and a mortgage.

c) Look to rent a larger house and ask one of your friends if they would like to share a home to spread out the cost of the rent.

Why is A incorrect? Sure, it's great that you have a house when many people don't, but if you refuse to take action or look at other potential opportunities, you'll always be stuck in a house that's too small for you and makes you miserable.

Why is C incorrect? You're avoiding the problem here; you're telling yourself that you're bad at saving, so you avoid having to do it. Plus, sharing with another person may also bring a myriad of other problems into the picture.

Why is B correct? You're taking control here. You're being sensible and looking for options that will allow you to buy your own house. Yes, you're taking out a loan, but you need to find an option that you can comfortably pay back every month. Make a budget and go for it!

What might come from taking the correct action? Provided you budget correctly and only take out a loan/mortgage for the amount you can afford, you will be able to buy your own home. Once it is paid off, you own that property. You now have freedom and a real sense of achievement!

Can you see how taking a small, calculated risk can open up a world of opportunities? You don't have to be gung-ho about taking chances; you can take small steps that make you feel comfortable. The point is that you're moving forward and seeing what is possible rather than assuming that some things are simply not for you.

Get Out Of Your Comfort Zone

We stay in our comfort zones because they're, well, comfortable. They don't make us feel nervous or anxious; we know what we're doing, and we're happy where we are.

But what is your comfort zone doing for you?

Life is for living. That doesn't mean you jump out of planes or bungee jump off tall buildings for the hell of it—unless you want to, of course—but it does mean that you're willing to see where opportunities take you. If it works out, great! If not, you tried, and you might learn something along the way.

Remember, it doesn't always work out the first time, but what we learn helps us adjust our mindset and approach, and we can make a success of it the next time.

A great way to build the confidence to break out of your comfort zone is to use positive affirmations and mantras.

You might wonder how telling yourself positive things actually makes you believe them. Well, it's not magic, but it's something very close to it. You see, the human brain learns by repetition. It's one of the reasons why your teacher in pre-school made you recite the alphabet in a song over and over again. It commits it to your memory. The magical thing here is that when you constantly tell yourself positive things, it affects your entire outlook over time and makes you more positive overall.

"If you don't like something, change it. If you can't change it, change your attitude." – Maya Angelou

A positive mantra or affirmation can be anything you want it to be; they're one and the same regardless of whether you choose to call it a mantra or an affirmation. It's just a statement that relates to something you want to truly believe, and you repeat it several times every day until your brain takes it on as truth.

Exercise 12: Creating a Positive Affirmation/Mantra

What do you want to believe? Think about that for a second.

Do you want to become more positive in general? Do you want to truly feel your own self-worth? Do you want to believe that you can lose weight or change your job?

Think about what you really want to program your brain to believe for a second. You can use several affirmations at any one time, but at the start, it's best to stick to just one so you don't confuse yourself.

So, let's say that you want to be more positive.

A positive affirmation could be, "I am a positive person who sees the light everywhere I go."

Now, you might not believe it right now, but the more you say it, the more you will!

If you want to focus on your self-worth, you could use something like, "I am worthy; I am strong."

Write down a few positive affirmations/mantras here, and shortlist down to the first one you want to focus on:

_____

_____

_____

_____

_____

_____

_____

_____

_____

_____

_____

_____

_____

_____

_____

_____

_____

_____

_____

_____

_____

_____

Now that you've chosen your affirmation, how do you use it? Follow these easy steps:

- Write your affirmation down on a sticky note and leave it somewhere visible, such as the bathroom mirror, on your computer monitor, or setting it as your phone background. This will ensure you see the affirmation regularly.
- When you wake up in the morning, take a deep breath, close your eyes, and repeat the affirmation three times.
- As you say the words, visualize yourself feeling exactly how you want to feel.
- Repeat the process several times throughout the day and any time that you notice your confidence is wavering or you're facing a difficult situation.

You won't notice results overnight, but in a short amount of time, you'll see the effects coming your way.

In addition to affirmations and mantras, you can try reframing as well. Whenever you notice that you're having a negative thought, quicky flip it on its head and turn it into something positive.

For example, if you think to yourself, "I look fat in this outfit," stop and tell yourself that you're thinking negatively. Then, change it to something positive, such as "This outfit really shows off my curves." The more you do it, the more positive you'll become!

Chapter Five

Self-Care Isn't Selfish

"Self-care is not self-indulgence; it is self-preservation." – Audre Lorde

One of the most feared human traits is selfishness. We all go out of our way to try and avoid people seeing us as selfish because we don't want others to think badly of us, but we have somehow forgotten that self-care is vitally important. It doesn't mean that you're being selfish.

How can it be selfish to put yourself first and look after your own needs?

It doesn't mean that you're not thinking about anyone else in your life at all; it means that you're adding fuel to your own car (metaphorically speaking), so you have the energy to continue helping others, too. After all, if you don't look after yourself, you're not going to be able to do anything for anyone else in your life, either. Burnout is a real thing.

So, repeat after me: "Self-care isn't selfish!" Say it loud and proud!

The benefits of self-are are far-reaching and can't be ignored, and self-care is said to reduce the chances of anxiety and depression, boost one's mood in general, increase happiness, help you develop resilience, improve relationships, and help you make strong decisions.

Not bad, right?

The problem is that most people feel uncomfortable focusing on themselves at first. But like any habit, the more you do it, the easier it will become. And trust me—you'll start to love it.

Self-Care Sunday

It doesn't have to be a Sunday, it can be any day of the week, but you need to schedule one day out of every single week that you decide to engage in self-care only. That doesn't mean that the other six days are focused on other people, but it does mean that you have a full day of self-enjoyment.

You need it.

So, what should you do during your self-care day? Basically, anything that makes you feel good and all the things you enjoy. And you don't get to feel bad about it, either!

Exercise 13: Filling Your Self-Care Day

All too often, we give up our spare time and energy to other people and don't realize how much it's taking out of us. It's only when you think back that you realize that you no longer do certain activities that you used to love. Well, no more of that! Your self-care day can be solely for those things.

In the space below, write down anything that you love to do but no longer have the time for or anything that you used to enjoy, but your time spent on those activities fell by the wayside as life became too busy.

Look at that list—can you see how much of your time and energy you give to other people? It's time to take some of it back. Your self-care day, whatever day of the week you have chosen, should be dedicated to the things on that list. You don't have to do all of them at once, but use that list as a source of inspiration when you want to do something for yourself.

Of course, your self-care day should also include things like eating your favorite foods, relaxing, watching your favorite TV shows, and pampering. Basically, treat yourself like you would your best friend because that's what you should be to yourself.

Exercise 14: Tracking Your 'Me' Time

If you're not sure about what you can do in your self-care time or what makes you feel good, it's time to test the waters.

For the next week, keep a journal and write down five things you did for yourself each day for every day of the week. If you struggle to come up with five, well, that should tell you something—but do try.

Once you've got your weekly results, sit down and question how those things made you feel.

For instance, if you baked yourself a cake, how did that make you feel? Not just the eating part but the process of actually making it for yourself.

If you went out for a walk with the dog, how did you feel during the walk? Did you feel relaxed and calm?

Choose the exercises or small tasks that make you feel the best and incorporate them into your daily routine more and more.

And remember: *You have permission to look after yourself and put your own interests first. You give yourself that permission because it matters.*

It's Time To Be Thankful

"Acknowledging the good that you already have in your life is the foundation for all abundance." – Eckhart Tolle

It's very easy to forget all the wonderful things you have in life. We all do it; we get so caught up in the rigors of daily life that we start to focus on the things we wish we had, and we lose sight of all the things right in front of us.

Taking things for granted is a human condition, but that doesn't mean it's something you should allow to become a habit in your own life. Of course, it's normal to wish you had this, that, or the other, but it shouldn't become an obsession. That's when materialism becomes toxic.

Turning your attention back to the wonderful things you already have in your life helps you to see that you're in pretty good shape already. It doesn't mean there isn't work to be done, but you can see that perhaps your life isn't as bad as you thought.

This is called **gratitude**, and living a more grateful life can:

- Help you deal with difficult times more easily
- Allow you to develop a positive mindset
- Help you to relish positive experiences in life rather than allowing them to pass you by
- Help to improve your mental health by boosting your mood
- Allow you to build stronger relationships with those around you

So, what are you grateful for?

Exercise 15: Gratitude Journal

It's not easy to pick out of thin air the things you're grateful for in life, but a gratitude journal will help you to see that you have more in your life than you might realize.

For two weeks, keep a gratitude journal and write in it three things you're grateful for every single day. It's a good idea to sit down in the evening and think back over your day to come up with your entries.

After two weeks, look over the journal and see how many wonderful things and experiences you have in your life. You'll realize that it's the small things that breed happiness, and you'll know what you need to do more of to bring even more joy into your life.

Mindfulness Meditation & How it Can Help You

Another thing that can make it hard to realize what you have in your life—and can make it hard to focus on self-care in general—is a tendency to not live in the moment.

Are you always thinking back to the past or jumping ahead to the future? For sure, there's nothing wrong with having goals and desires for the future, but if you allow them to completely take over the here and now, are you really living?

Basically, no, you're not.

It's important to be in the moment and to make the present as beautiful and enjoyable as it can be. The past is gone; you can't change what you did or didn't do, or what anyone else did or didn't do, for that matter. By focusing on what has already gone, all you're doing is making your present miserable. It's pointless, isn't it?

Instead, learn from your mistakes in the past, whether that's something you did and wish you hadn't or something you didn't do and you wish you had. Use the past as a way to educate yourself for the present.

In the space below, write down anything from your past that you often ruminate on:

_____
_____
_____
_____
_____
_____
_____
_____
_____
_____
_____
_____
_____
_____
_____
_____
_____
_____
_____
_____

Okay, now, what can you do about those things? Is there something you can do now to make the present better, or is there a lesson you can learn?

_____

_____

_____

_____

_____

_____

_____

_____

_____

_____

_____

_____

_____

_____

_____

_____

_____

_____

_____

_____

_____

_____

_____

_____

_____

_____

_____

_____

This quick exercise should help you to see that thinking back to the past is only useful if you're going to learn something from it to make the present even better. Otherwise, it's nothing short of a waste of time—unless you have a time machine, of course.

Thinking about the future too much is also problematic. It's normal to have dreams and desires and to work toward achieving them, but becoming obsessive about them and making the present all about those things means you're missing the good stuff.

"Mindfulness is awareness without criticism or judgment." – Jan Chozen Bays

This is where mindfulness medication can help you.

Mindfulness basically means that you learn to stay in the present moment and appreciate the small things that make it wonderful. You're able to understand what is going on around you without jumping to conclusions, disaster thinking, or being negative about the whole thing; instead, you observe and take it all in.

When you learn to be mindful, you're calm, collected, and can handle whatever life throws at you. And guess what? It makes you more positive, too. It's the ultimate form of self-care.

So, how do you do it?

Learning to be present in the moment isn't easy and won't happen for you straightaway, but practice makes perfect. Try this next exercise on a regular basis to start your mindfulness journey.

Exercise 16: Walking Mindfulness Meditation

It's very easy to be distracted by every tiny thing, be it your cell phone, social media, traffic, general noise, or intrusive thoughts. This walking mindfulness meditation exercise will help you to shut all of that out and focus on the here and now.

- Head outside for a walk alone. Leave your cell phone at home or put it on silent mode in your bag. Don't leave it on vibrate mode if it's in your pocket, as it will only continue to distract you.

- When you're ready, take a few deep breaths to calm your mind.

- Turn your attention to one detail in your surroundings as you're walking. It could be a tree or a field, or even a dog running around.

- Now, really focus on that one element you've chosen and zone in on the small details. For instance, if it's a tree, think about the strong trunk extending into the ground or the vibrant green of the leaves. Go through every detail you can see before moving on to another element.

- If you feel like you're getting distracted at any point, take a breath or two and focus your mind. Push any thoughts away and tell yourself you'll deal with them later.

- Repeat the exercise until you've covered all things you can see or you're tired. You should try to stay in this meditation for at least 20 minutes.

- When you're ready, take a few breaths and slowly return to your walk without focusing on anything.

The more you practice mindfulness, the more you'll be able to stick with it as your usual pace of life. You could also try mindful eating, which means you really focus on the food you're eating, the tastes and textures, and slowing down your chewing to feel every sensation. The more you focus on small details such as this, the easier mindfulness will be.

Chapter Six

Toxicity is Toxic

"Letting go of toxic people in your life is a big step in loving yourself." –
Hussein Nishah

You can't control the world around you; you can only control your reaction to it. That doesn't only mean what you do in response to problems and feelings but also choosing your company wisely.

Toxicity will ruin any attempt you make to improve your life from the inside out. If you continue to surround yourself with people who always seem intent on dragging you down, you might as well forget any changes you're attempting to make. They won't work because the toxicity thrown at you by other people will counteract your efforts.

For that reason, it's time to take a life inventory.

Now, I understand that cutting people out of your life is hard, and in some cases, not even possible, but the acknowledgment of toxicity and then making an attempt to manage it is important.

For instance, maybe you've got a friend who always makes you feel bad about yourself. They're always using gaslighting techniques, or they make comments that are often backhanded and make you question your own worth or appearance. Now, firstly, that's not a friend, but you might still feel awkward about cutting them out of your life.

It's understandable, but what is more important to you: the friendship or your self-worth?

You might also have a colleague who often tries to take credit for the work you do or makes comments to make you question your abilities. Of course, you can't cut a colleague out of your life because you have to work alongside them, but you can minimize the amount of contact you have with them.

That's what we're going to explore in this chapter.

You Are Who You Spend Your Time With

The people you surround yourself influence so much about your life and how you feel about yourself. It's not just toxic friends or colleagues that can affect you, but bad relationships, too. Sometimes, you can love someone, but they're simply not good for you.

If you want to change your life, it's not only about you but also about what is around you. But then, the responsibility to change that falls on your lap.

Exercise 17: What Are Your Toxic Influences?

It's time to do some serious reflection, and some of this may not be easy. In the space below, write down anything or anyone who makes you feel bad about yourself and who you suspect may be a toxic influence. It doesn't have to be a person; it can also be a thing, such as a bad working environment.

_____

_____

_____

_____

_____

_____

_____

_____

_____

_____

_____

_____

_____

_____

_____

_____

_____

_____

_____

_____

_____

_____

Now, take each person or thing you've written down and create a pros and cons list of them being in your life. Doing this will help you explore whether or not this person or thing deserves space in your life or not.

Pros:

_____

_____

_____

_____

_____

_____

_____

_____

_____

_____

_____

_____

_____

_____

_____

_____

_____

_____

_____

_____

_____

_____

_____

Cons:

_____

_____

_____

_____

_____

_____

_____

_____

_____

_____

_____

_____

_____

_____

_____

_____

_____

_____

_____

_____

_____

_____

_____

_____

_____

The point to remember here is that nobody and nothing is 100% perfect. There will be cons for every single entry on your list, but the point is whether or not there are more pros than cons. If there are, great! You can manage this. If not, it's time to move on to the next section and question what you should do next.

Managing The Pain of Toxicity

"You never fully see how toxic someone is until you breathe fresher air." –

Unknown

Cutting someone out of your life or even realizing that they're toxic and not the best for you isn't going to be without pain. You might already know deep down that this person has toxic traits that affect your self-confidence and self-belief, but you keep pushing it down because you don't want to face it or upset them.

The thing is, you have to focus on yourself here. If a person is hell-bent on making you feel negative, you have to question whether they have your best interests in mind. Maybe they don't realize they're doing it, and in that case, a simple conversation might solve the problem. However, people who often resort to toxic tactics often know exactly what they're doing. These tactics include:

- Passive aggressive behavior and comments
- Condescending remarks
- Gaslighting
- Manipulation
- Excessive demands
- Abuse
- Betrayal
- Disparaging remarks designed to make you feel bad
- Dragging you down to make themselves feel better
- Never being there for you

Do you really need this in your life?

Of course, you don't, but if you have a long-standing 'friendship' with this person or you've been in a relationship with them for a while, simply cutting them out will hurt you in the process. What you have to remember is that while it might sting for a while, you will get through it, and in the end, you'll be glad you did it.

Three Options: Which Will You Choose?

When you identify a person as toxic, you have three options:

- Cut them out
- Minimize contact
- Reframe the situation

Let's take a look at how each option works and use the example of a toxic friend who always makes you feel bad about yourself with disparaging remarks, and they're never there for you when you need them.

- **Cut them out** – You decide that you no longer want to take part in this friendship, and you cut all contact. You block them on social media and do not reply to any contact attempts they make. Prior to doing this, you would need to have a conversation and explain your actions, refusing to listen when they try to tell you that you're wrong.
- **Minimize contact** – You still see your friend, but not as much as before; you also minimize what they can see on your social media platforms by applying filters. You are polite with them, but you don't reveal as much about your life as before. As such, you adjust your expectations of the friendship.

- **Reframe the situation** – Acknowledge that this person isn't a great friend but also realize that you have shared many great experiences in the past and you have many memories of your time together. When this person starts to act negatively toward you, you walk away and set boundaries on what you will and won't put up with.

As you can see, you can use this process in any type of toxic situation in your life. It's easy to just say that you need to cut them out, but it's not always possible. Maybe you have mutual friends, you work together, or it's a family member who is quite close to everyone else in your home.

Choosing the best option will allow you to side-step toxicity and discover peace in your life.

Exercise 18: Choose Your Route to Free Yourself From Toxicity

From the list of toxic people or things that you identified earlier in this chapter, which of the three options suits the situations best? Spend some time exploring each choice and go with the one that feels best to you.

However, don't assume that moving away from a situation or even minimizing contact will be easy on you at first. If you need to rely upon close friends to help you, do so.

This is especially the case if you're moving away from a toxic relationship that you've invested a lot of time and love into. Some people find they need professional help in such situations, and if that's the case for you, go for it. It will be the best decision you ever make.

The Art of Saying "No"

"It's only by saying 'no' that you can concentrate on the things that are really important." – Steve Jobs

How often do you say "yes" in a day? Really think about that for a second. It's probably quite a few times.

We often don't want to say "no" to the people around us because we don't want them to think that we're not being helpful or that we can't handle what we already have on our plate. The truth is, by constantly saying "yes," you're simply adding to the stress you already have, and people will continue to take advantage of your good nature.

The truth is that saying "no" when you need to or want to is healthy. Of course, don't go around refusing to do everything simply because you can; but if you really feel that you don't have time to do something for someone, or you seriously don't want to and it's not something you're duty-bound to do, feel free to say "no" politely and don't feel the need to explain yourself.

Taking on too much is one of the key causes of stress and eventual burnout. None of that is fun.

Exercise 19: The "No" Challenge

It could be that you don't realize how many times per day you say "yes," and how much extra pressure you're putting on yourself. So, it's time to take part in a challenge!

Every single day, challenge yourself to say "no" at least once. Make sure that you choose an opportunity that is wise and worthy; don't just say "no" for the sake of doing so.

At the end of the day, think about how saying "no" felt to you. Did it feel awkward at first? Is it getting easier as the days go by? Is saying "no" giving you more time for yourself or helping you to prioritize your time better?

"You are not required to set yourself on fire to keep others warm." – Unknown

Learning how to say "no" helps you to set boundaries against those people who are willing to take advantage of your good nature. Unfortunately, there are many people in the world who are happy to do just that. When you start to say "no," you take the power away from them and keep it in your own hands. You choose when you agree to do something for them, and very soon, they'll start to realize that they can no longer take you for granted as they used to do.

It's not pleasant when you realize that people in your life might not be as true as you thought they were; it's a hard lesson to learn. However, it's a lesson that will enhance your life once you understand what you need to do to overcome the toxicity they bring.

Chapter Seven

Change Is Scary, But Staying the Same Is Worse

"Your life does not get better by chance; it gets better by change." – Jim Rohn

Nobody likes change. It causes us to move away from our comfort zones and face things that we're not sure of. You'll probably never reach the point in your life where you love change and want to face it daily. If you do, you probably don't even need this workbook!

But you can reach the point where you face change with less anxiety than before, and from there, you can embrace the positive elements it brings because, really, change is a positive thing. It's easy to see it as terrifying and a journey into the unknown, but there are amazing things to be found past the point of what you already know.

Who knows the people you might meet and what they may become to you? What about the potential opportunities the change may bring and their power to change your life?

Start to see change as something exciting and mysterious rather than something to always be feared. After all, every change you face has the power to change your life in amazing ways.

Pushing Back Against Change is Natural

If the news of an impending change, or a sudden change happening out of the blue, makes you want to kick into defense mode and push back against it, don't worry; that's a normal reaction. It's actually your brain trying to keep you safe, even though, in reality, there's nothing to fear.

But just because it's a normal reaction doesn't mean you should allow it to continue, though. Life is scary sometimes; it's part of what makes it so much fun! But as scary as change can be, it's scarier to avoid change because it means your life will always remain as it is now. You'll be stuck, unable to move in any direction. I'm assuming that's not what you want because you picked up this book for help!

If you want to improve your life and bring new energy and opportunities toward you, it's important to bravely step toward change and explore it rather than automatically running away or trying to fight it. This is one of those moments in life when you really can say that if you don't try, you'll never know what might have come your way.

Don't you want to find out?

The Story of The Angel & The Devil

"We cannot become what we want by remaining what we are." – Max Depree

When you face a change and become anxious or fearful of what might happen, you may experience the metaphorical angel and the devil on your shoulder.

Don't worry; they're not actually real. It's just the internal tussle between being fearful and running away and being brave enough to step into your power and go for what you want instead.

The angel wants you to bravely step forward toward a new opportunity and tries to give you the pep talk you need to take baby steps toward where you need to be, but the devil has other ideas!

The devil wants you to give in to fear and stay where you are. It's a negative force that feeds into your worries, and if you listen, it will keep you stuck.

The next time you're facing a change or problem of any kind, tune into the angel on your shoulder and try to mute the devil. You'll notice this voice as a limiting and damaging force that tells you that you "can't" do things or that you "shouldn't." But the angel will be a lot more soothing and will tell you that "You don't know until you try" or "You're stronger than you think."

Always listen to the angel. The devil is simply tapping into your fears and feeding off of whatever you're most scared of. But the thing we already know about fears? They're not real; they're an illusion that, more often than not, never comes to fruition. So, in effect, you're avoiding facing a possibly wonderful change in your life because you're focusing on something that's not even real.

Quite strange when you think about it, right?

Exercise 20: Muting The Devil

So, how can you turn the volume down on the devil and turn the angel's voice up higher? Visualization can help.

- Picture the negative voice in your head as a black ball of toxicity. It might help to picture it pulsating, to give it a sense of realness.
- Hold it in your hands and feel its heavy weight. How does it feel?

- Tell the ball that it's negative and you want nothing to do with it.

- Take a breath and imagine yourself squeezing the ball in your hands until it's so small that you can squeeze it into just one fist.

- As you crush it in your hand, feel the ball becoming lighter and slowly stop pulsating.

- Then, throw it as far away as possible, with as much force as you can muster.

- As you throw, say the words, "I will not listen to you."

- Zone in on the positive voice in your head—what is it saying to you now?

You can use this exercise whenever you're trying to face a new situation or opportunity and are second-guessing yourself or allowing "what if" or "I can't" thoughts to take over.

Dare To Dream

"The distance between dreams and reality is called action." – Brian Tracy

What do you really want to achieve in your life?

If you haven't got a bucket list, you really should create one! In the space below, scribble down a few things that you really want to achieve, no matter how achievable you might think they are right now.

_____

_____

_____

_____

_____

_____

_____

_____

_____

_____

_____

_____

_____

_____

_____

_____

_____

_____

_____

_____

_____

_____

_____

_____

_____

_____

Have you made any progress toward achieving any of those entries? If not, why not?

It's likely to be because you're scared of taking a chance or that it seems like too lofty a goal.

The thing is, everything seems like a mountain to climb when you're standing at the bottom, looking up. What you need to do is break the journey down into more manageable chunks. Then, with every chunk you achieve, celebrate, and move on to the next one. You'll soon be at the summit.

When your self-belief is at an all-time low, and you don't have a whole lot of confidence, achieving goals seems like a major ask. As such, you'll likely procrastinate to avoid what you are convinced will be a major failure. But what if it's not?

I know "what if" thoughts aren't the best, but when they're positive, I say use them!

"What if it works?"

"What if I make it?"

Explore those thoughts and allow yourself to dream a little. Visualize what it feels like to reach your goals. It's not just daydreaming; it's a strategy that can actually bring major results. When you have visualized actually achieving something, you have experience—albeit in another realm—but it still means you have experience, and you can use that to go forth and get what you want.

Exercise 21: A Seat At The Table

The dreams you want to make a reality don't need to be huge things; they can be anything you want. This is your life, after all. However, for this exercise, choose the dream you want the most right now and concentrate on that. You can go back and repeat this exercise for the other dreams and goals on your list, but for now, choose one to avoid confusing or overwhelming yourself.

So, what is the dream? Write it down here:

_____

_____

_____

_____

_____

_____

_____

_____

_____

_____

_____

_____

_____

_____

_____

_____

_____

_____

_____

_____

_____

_____

_____

_____

_____

_____

_____

Imagine your dream as a statue or something else that is easy for you to visualize in your mind. Imagine it sat at a table with you, and you're about to enjoy dinner together. In this picture, you're on good terms with your dream.

Ask your dream what you need to do to start making progress toward achieving it. From what comes to you during this exercise, fill in the table below. Use one line for each milestone/chunk of action to move toward your final outcome.

Dream	Action to take	Potential problems & how to overcome them	Timescale to achieve

But it's not good enough to simply write down what you need to do, though—you need to take the actions and move through them!

Planning something is easy, but actually putting the plan into action is the hard part. That's why your first action should be the easiest one; it gives you the confidence you need to keep moving forward because you've already taken one step on the road.

Fear and confusion will only fuel procrastination. Before you know it, you'll keep putting your next action off, and you'll never get around to it. The longer it goes on, the more you'll simply assume that it's not worth going after your dream anymore, but it's simply that you didn't commit to the process and go for it.

In the end, you only have yourself to blame, and *you* have to live with that disappointment.

Is that what you want?

Of course not! That's what brought you to read this book in the first place. So, commit to the changes you need to make and be brave enough to go after them.

Pitfalls On The Way

"Life isn't about finding yourself. Life is about creating yourself." – George Bernard Shaw

Whenever you work toward achieving anything, you're bound to face a few challenges along the way. Change tends to do that; it likes to test you and see how strong you are or how much you want what you're working toward. Don't let the obstacles win!

Instead of seeing problems as failures or a reason to give up, use them as learning opportunities instead. What do you need to change your approach and do something that allows you to overcome the issue? What new skills can you learn to give you a stronger chance of success? Do you need to change direction or simply tweak something minor?

Your attitude toward challenges will shape whether or not you reach your goals. So, rather than fearing them, welcome them and see them as something that has the power to transform your life for the better.

Because they do.

You'll surprise yourself the more you push on. You'll see what you can achieve, and you'll realize that it's a lot more than you consider yourself capable of right now. With every chunk or milestone you achieve, you'll gain confidence; and with every challenge you overcome, you'll grow in self-belief.

When you mute the devil on your shoulder and tune into the angel, everything gets better, and you no longer fear change. Instead, you say, "Bring it on!"

Conclusion

"You were born to be real, not perfect." - Unknown

Well done! You've reached the end of the workbook, and you should be feeling full of confidence and excitement about the new journey you're about to embark upon.

Learning to love yourself is a life-long road. But the sooner you start, the faster you'll grab the benefits.

From time to time, events might cause you to take a step backward, but that's okay. At the end of the day, you're human and not immune to life's ups and downs. What matters the most is how you bounce back stronger than before and learn the lessons you're supposed to take on board.

You'll never be perfect. That's something you need to make peace with because what is perfect? What one person sees as perfect is totally different from another. You don't want to be chasing validation for the rest of your days, so make peace with who you are and work to learn from everything that comes your way. By doing that, you'll always keep moving forward, and you'll never find yourself stuck or moving backward again.

Remember, you'll have good days and bad days because you're human. There will be times when you don't make a whole lot of progress, but there will also be days when you're ticking things off your to-do list like the wind.

Celebrate the good days and be kind to yourself on the bad days. In fact, be kind to yourself on ALL days!

So, now you've worked through the book, what are your next steps? What points are you going to start ticking off to move forward? Scribble down some thoughts below.

_____

_____

_____

_____

_____

_____

_____

_____

_____

_____

_____

_____

_____

_____

_____

_____

_____

_____

_____

_____

_____

_____

_____

Choose one and get started! What's stopping you?

"If you have the ability to love, love yourself first." – *Charles Bukowski*

Self-love is such an important part of a happy and healthy life. Do you remember the last time you smiled so hard your face hurt? Or when you laughed so much that your ribs ached?

Self-love gives that ability back to you.

But first, you need to get up and get moving. From this second forward, don't allow fear to hold you back. It's nothing but an illusion, anyway. Mute the devil on your shoulder and focus on the whispers from the angel instead. It will never steer you in the wrong direction, but the devil most certainly will.

In the space below, write down any positive or motivational thoughts and ideas you have right now or that you've had throughout reading this workbook. When you feel you need a boost of confidence, read them back, and you'll feel instantly uplifted.

_____

_____

_____

_____

_____

_____

_____

_____

_____

_____

_____

_____

_____

_____

_____

_____

_____

_____

_____

_____

_____

_____

_____

_____

_____

_____

_____

_____

_____

_____

_____

_____

_____

_____

_____

And remember, the only person who can take this journey is YOU.

YOU have the power to change your life. YOU have the power to achieve whatever you put your mind to, and YOU have the final say in how other people make you feel.

For now, it's time for me to bid you goodbye. You now have all the tools you need to make positive and lasting changes in your life. The first step might be the hardest, but from there, you'll find that putting one foot in front of the other becomes easier with every single step.

Good luck!

A Short Message from Cameron:

Being a small author, reviews play a crucial role in supporting my journey! I would greatly appreciate it if you could take a moment to leave a review for my book.

If you found this book enjoyable and it resonated with you, I humbly ask that you consider sharing your thoughts and rating. Your contribution can make a difference in helping others discover my work 😊

To leave a review conveniently, simply scan the QR code below with your camera!

It won't take more than a few seconds and will help me out tremendously.

Thank you, I can't wait to read what you thought of my book!

Made in the USA
Middletown, DE
08 January 2025

69120879R00055